Vogue 3:16

This collection is just the beginning of my testimony. This is me trying to explain my faith and my hope that this world is not only full of monochromatic dark and light. This is how I came to love myself. I gave up one part of who I am, so that another part could live.

5/3/15 14

→

What year is
this anyways?!!

Denise,

Thank you for supporting
my heArt.

(signature)

WRAGSINK. PUBLISHING COMPANY
Sharon Hill, PA 19079

Cover Art by GG Photography – ggphotography917@gmail.com
Cover Design by Holly Haines – hollyhaines@gmail.com

wragsink@gmail.com
www.wragsink.com

Printed in the United States of America

Acknowledgments

I used to wonder why authors thanked their publishers and editors. I thought to myself, "Those folks aren't family." But they are. They become family. The good ones become so invested in your work, their feelings are a little hurt when you neglect it.

They're looking forward to your book more than you are. You speak nonchalantly about it. They speak with enthusiasm. You're tired of looking at this shit; they can't wait to get their hands on it.

These old ass poems. These new ones you can't make up your mind about. These old ones you've remixed and combined with other lost and found scraps of wtf in your corridors... You don't even know when you wrote half of this shit.

But when you've made your final edits...you don't email your sister. Don't email your relatives... You email your publisher first. No one has been rooting for you more than them... Not just because they've made a financial investment, but because they believe in you. They're invested in the change your work can make and will do everything in their power to make it happen!

Then you email your editors.

You might have missed something. And those folks could catch hell fire if it were thrown at them...imagine what they can do with a few grammatical errors...with a concept that is just a smidge off. And most of my editors have gone unpaid. They are mostly close friends who love me and appreciate my work. They are my polishers.

Thank you to the people who answered the phone and read all those emails I sent out. Thank you to my publishing and editing family. I don't have a specific poem for you, because you are the marrow in their bones.

To my SDSU Vaginas, thank you for giving. Your lives and stories lay protected in this cage of ribs.

To the people I met in San Diego: You carved through my excuses, then filled me with love & light. I learned from your greatness. I carry it in my heart. To Las Vegas, thank you for the perfect welcome. To life...to my family for being resilience personified, thank you.

Being a writer is an interesting thing. Balancing silence with foreground noise. Being a spoken word poet, even worse. Balancing introversion with commanding the attention of an audience. To be a spoken word artist on page...attempting to dance in the ashes of forever in your very own book.

Pretty cool.

Poetry

Sometimes I Forget To Breathe

Sometimes fears sink their canines into my tongue
My stomach is overcome
bulldozed by doubt
Angst weighs in the pit beneath my lower eyelid
and I am lucky to even get out my heart's prayer

This physical space always feels cramped and borrowed
I am always too wide
Too loud
Too presumptuous
Zealous
A well, overflowed with wishes

When the person I loved most
showed me the sonogram
that would end our relationship
I cried joy for his happiness
not the loss of our future

I have picked up burning hot skillets
with bare hands
and focused only on transferring food to plate

I taught myself how to stifle coughs
so people would never notice me choking

I tend to concern myself with invisibility
To stop breathing so loudly
To order the least expensive item on the menu

To enter rooms in silence
and sneak into a modest corner

In my twenty-six years worth of infinite wisdom
I've become a professional
at telling myself & God what I don't deserve
God provides blessings, I play hard to give
This behavior…
This life…
I'm glad God is persistent

I have to remember
I have done what others wouldn't
I have shared worlds within five-minute-moments
Others may not understand why I give so much
But it is always worth it

I have to tell myself,
"Carry on, sister-girl. Carry on."

No matter where I am
there is a place I belong

I deserve to be loved
Deserve to be forgiven
Deserve to be well-fed
Bedded well

And by deserve, I mean I don't
deserve any of this more than the next
human being sucking air

At the very least, I deserve to be thankful

Remember, in the early 80's, two children
put their hands together and the only thing
they asked God to give them
was a little sister

I have to remember
I am the product of the prayers of children
I am enough
I am here on purpose
And the reason this physical space
always feels cramped
and borrowed
is because the only place I've ever belonged
is in the heart of an earnest prayer

The Mission

I write to clear out the cobwebs
that cover the fragile surfaces of my mind
I write for clear blue skies
and "sunshine, on a cloudy day"

I write to remember what hope feels like
To pay homage to people I've forgotten
For people who have given me stories I've never deserved
For friends unafraid of creating another family
and accepting me in it

For sacrifice in the raw
For the woman I will one day become

I write my poems for people who deserve them:

Like my grandmother—
Who refuses to pass away
until she feels like we no longer need her

My sister—
Whose heart is made out of glass
beautiful when it catches the sunlight
smooth to the touch
dangerous when broken

My cousin—
Who at 16 was paying bills
buying groceries, and raising his nephew

While his grandmother surrendered to Alzheimer's
and no one even noticed

For my younger cousin —
Who had the courage to speak
at his own mother's funeral
and didn't shed a single tear

For Nicole Mehta —
A woman who acts as her own compass
and has taught me how to respect others
exactly as they are

For Mani and Danielle —
Who remind me of how much poetry
has changed my life

For Francine Cepeda Blacksher —
Who cannot have a conversation
without uplifting my spirit to God
for freedom

For Ant Black —
Whose first poetry album still leaves me full
He says, "God's not finished with me yet
so I am Unmastered."

For Rudy Francisco —
Whose passionate ambition always makes me question
whether I can give poetry the commitment it deserves

For Viet Mai –
Who is secretly teaching me how to say "no"

For Jessica Molina –
A constant gardener pruning away at her insecurities
scouring her feelings for purity
the same way she scours her kitchen counters

For Christopher Wilson—
Who stood by my side
the first time I performed at an open mic

I perform to remind myself that I am amazing
because sometimes I forget
when I'm not onstage

This is for my God
How in all things I do, I try to acknowledge Him
How my clarity and inspiration
never ceases to come from Him

How I've denied Him more than thrice
And He's never denied me
His love

Sometimes I Comb My Hair - Poem

I'm pretty sure my hair and combs
have always been adversaries
with my ears and someone's hands
caught in the cross-fire
Whether it was the pressing comb who scalded
the side of my ear or regular combs,
who often & impolitely broke off in my hair
There were always casualties of the ongoing war

These days, doing my hair
really just depends on my patience level
My hair is extremely thick; it takes hours to be tamed
And perms? HA! Perms have a limited effect on my hair
So I've decided that my hair is victorious
and I will allow it to "BE"

Now when you see me it will *be* braided
or it will *be* in a natural state
and you can love it, or leave it alone

Cause Maya Angelou said,
"I've learned that people will forget what you said,
people will forget what you did, but people will never forget
how you made them feel."

Remember the way I make you feel
I want people to remember me for my demeanor
not for the hair on my head
(I am an all-over-the-place Black woman,
my hair is subject to infinite change)

Please don't try to judge me solely based upon my hairstyle

Understand that:
My afro, as wondrous as it was, did not make me
"Afrocentric"
My locks, as glorious as they were, did not transform me
into an aware-reggae-listening-marijuana-smoking-sistah
My decision to get my hair braided into individuals
did not mean I felt a deep sense of regret
for cutting all of my damn hair off
And when my hair is short,
it does not make me any less of a woman

It means I am a risk-taker
It means I have comfort and confidence
in my inner and outer essence
to surpass society's suppressive view of "classic beauty"

So many young ladies suffer
from low self-esteem
anorexia
bulimia
all because they want to fit
into the mold of what beauty is in America

But I have found my own undying cure:
Looking to individuals for their own beauty
Seeking out their passions
Respecting their strengths and weaknesses
and accepting them as children of God

I encourage you to do the same
8

Please Stop Advertising Ways
to Take Away My Flavor

There are billboards clouding San Diego skylines
like smog pollutes Los Angeles
They read "Diets don't work, the Lapband does!
1-800-Get-Thin"
My initial reaction, "fuck you mass media!"

If I am subjected to the disgusting photos
solely focused on increasing the visibility
of the female pelvic bone
via the pages of magazines
online networking sites
television commercials
my own email account
or by a 14' by 48' foot billboard
one. more. time.
I'm going to scream

I don't wanna fit into your "skinny jeans"
It's bad enough the jeans that fit my body
don't fit into my budget
I have to take what I can get

So no, I don't wanna go on the Oprah-
Açaí-berries-no bananas-
celebrity-fit-club-
I-can't-believe-she-just-had-a-baby-
and-STILL-looks-that-good — diet!!

I don't wanna lose 400,000 pounds

in 7 minutes while the moon is full
and the vultures are circling
That shit don't sound safe

I'm busy trying to improve my health
as opposed to being concerned
with your prescription to inject myself
with silicone and magical weight loss syringes
like they're the cure to the AIDS epidemic
you've engineered to destroy the immune system
of my self-confidence

I will eat an apple a day
and hope it keeps your bullshit away

Cause I prefer to have my supple C's
Arms, which give a bit of an extra wave
so people will know how much I'll miss them
I like my mid-section
Hips, widespread
to mimic the shape of a pear
and made to ease the birth of my future
I'll keep my thick thighs
and slightly muscular calves
bringing a natural rhythm to my stride
that your diets could never provide

So from now on
I think you should start
giving me a closer look
because I am simply
delicious

Denture Love

I wanna be with you long enough
to notice newly formed moles on your face
and trace them back to our lineage

Long enough to sit on park benches
facing the calm ocean and have the sunset say
we are the most beautiful thing that it has ever witnessed

Long enough to fall asleep in the middle of the day
quilted beneath piles of unread newspapers

I wanna be with you long enough to accidentally
put on your prescription bi-focal glasses and still
see through them clearly
because of how well I know your perspective

Because one day
both our chests
will sag lower than we ever imagined

When hair starts and stops sprouting
in awkward places

When Bride of Frankenstein streaks of grey and white
stretch across the majority of my crown
and bald spots form landmarks on your scalp
showcasing places we've both seen and forgotten
but that's okay, because I'm ready for that

denture love

Yes, remove portions of our bodies
and place them in containers for cleansing
so we can be together in two places
at the same time –
the bedroom
and the bathroom!

I wanna pick out my first cane with you
We can go orthopedic shoe-shopping together

Baby, we can kick it old school
in wheel chairs
with baseball cards
attached to the spokes
of our wheels with clothespins
so we can make that rhythmic
clackety-clack sound
whenever we roll around

I wanna trace my arthritic fingers
along the varicose veins under
your desert cracked
and wrinkled flesh
until I find an oasis
in your cataract-filled eyes
and remain there

Nothing will obstruct our double vision
Our love will never be a mirage

One day we'll have a home
filled with things priceless and forgotten
and that old people smell
we'll never seem to notice

Synchronized hearing aids
will pick up our grandchildren's laughter
and we'll smile

Mouths just homes
for taste buds to retire in comfortably

Bones will creak
louder than the wooden floors we roll on

I wanna lead a life with you
where every small daily action I perform
is a testament to our love, tried and true
from giving you the extra pillow on the bed,
to plugging your nose when you snore
to sacrifice

One day we'll be old
and decaying
and the only things we'll be sure of
are our dentures
and our love

Use Your Words

Most of us begin our lives full of tears and screams
We are confused
We are in pain from doctors smacking our asses
We are pissed that someone has smushed our bodies
through a narrow passageway
out of the warm nurturing amniotic fluid
and into a place where our lungs must now expand
We inhale
We cry

The first time I babysat a newborn
I tried not to interact with her
(Babies make me uncomfortable
because they don't use words)
This child was sensitive to my movements and mood
She wanted me to smile, wanted me to give kisses & hugs
and she quickly cleared the room of its awkward silence
Babies have no problem expressing their needs
nor their discontent

Over time, we stop coddling our children
& force them to use their words
But crying is our purest form of communication
before we befuddle meaning
and convolute life with euphemisms
How did it transform into a sign of weakness?
It's like we've forgotten what crying is for
It is for absolute joy and clarity

For the father who has lost his daughter
For the man overflowing with rage
For the child who learns the wrath of her parents
after talking back
For the mother all out of baby wipes
whose child just over-pooped her diaper
For the death of Mufasa & your pet rock
For "Toy Story 3"
For onions and spilled milk
For the last Girl Scout cookie & an empty bag of M&Ms
For holey socks, double rainbows, and blue sky

I cried in the middle of a class
while discussing my dreams
because I realized that sitting in that seat
speaking with my professor
and graduation less than 2 weeks away
I was mere moments from being everything
I said I wanted to be when I grew up

I always cry the purest tears
at the sight of women in bridal gowns
Somewhere in the depth of my essence
I always feel hope
maybe her marriage will last
maybe they mean it
Maybe, if my best friend can connect
and commit to the love of his life
then one day I can have that too
Right?

I wrote a poem through tears and snot
in a dark closet
in my own empty apartment
(I don't know who the hell I was hiding from)
I don't even know if I hid because I was ashamed
I just felt weakened
I felt tired and weary
I felt like the moon was full
and my face was the beach
overcome by the rising tide
I felt like I was drowning in every emotion
I had locked away...

Crying is for humans
For the days we wonder if someone
will ever love us unconditionally
When I worry that no man will
ever find me desirable enough
I won't ever possess the qualifications to be called "wife"

Old betrayal left me molested & placed in foster care
Insecurities send fault lines through my speech patterns
But I still have friends who understand me
who will always love me

Before there are words
there is noise and there are tears
Parents become attuned to the intonation of their child's voice
I am becoming more comfortable
speaking this mother tongue in public

I cry often
I am unashamed
I am proof that God lives in all things
even a tiny drop of water falling from a child's eye

For Eryn (16)

Apparently, the manual on being a woman
reads like the back of a shampoo bottle:

Step 1: Find a man
Step 2: Keep 'em
Step 3: Make babies
Step 4: Raise 'em and take care of your man

Repeat steps 1-4 as necessary
by any means necessary
Boom, it's that simple

And so many women have become consumed
with passion or despair while in search of "the one"
we've forgotten how to nurture ourselves

As women, we have the ability to push
through pain to bring forth life
No one ever teaches us how to push
through the pain that brings a relationship to its end
It's just something we learn

Here are the vitamins I've taught myself to swallow
and some things I wish someone
would have told me when I turned 16:

1. You often have more power than you realize
   Some people will just do things to test your limits
   Find your voice and say "No"
   When a hand wanders without invitation, move it away

For the tough situations there's always mace, pepper spray, kubotons, and family (they all work)

2. The Lion King had a bit of wisdom tucked into it,
   "You can run from your past, or learn from it,"- Rafiki
   Learning takes less time than wishing
   you never made that mistake

Speaking of mistakes…

3. Hold the people you date to the same standards
   you hold your friends to
   A significant other should also be a significant friend

4. Being prepared always pays off: tampons and pads should
   be stocked in every purse or backpack you own
           Trust me, someone will need them

5. You may notice that more women than men will tell you
   that you are beautiful, radiant, intelligent, or kind
           Believe them

6. Surround yourself with loving people
   They can see you from a better angle than any mirror
           Believe me

7. When people tell you that you're sooooooooooo young
           Believe them

Because this world is your ocean
take off your shoes and get your feet wet
Build a boat and sail above it
let the wind be your guide

Take lessons
put on scuba gear
and explore how amazing it is

Lay out in the sand
and enjoy the warmth of the sun
Pick up a seashell, whisper a question
and listen for an answer

Let the moon be your DJ
The stars, your disco lights
and dance to the crashing of waves

Grab a plastic bucket
build a sandcastle
name it after a loved one who has passed
watch the tide wash it away
accept that all things are temporary…
except Love

I wish somebody would've told me:
If God is Love, then Love is abundant

We have love like mangoes in Belize
We should be tossing it back
and forth at each other freely
There will always be more

Aunt Juanita

I wanted you louder, younger
more of a confidant
but you stuck to being yourself
a stark example
of how God has always wanted me
to accept others as they are
and see their value
like you did

You were patient...you had to be
because you'd sit outside
and listen to my Gramma talk for hours
Your silence was the highlight of her day
She is notorious
She picks-prunes-delegates-criticizes...
while you mastered the complexity of simple

My Gramma always taught me to respect the power of words
Lately, they are all that I have
At twenty-five, I finally learned that volumes
more have been written in silence
than in the number of journals
I've used as sounding boards
I have finally learned how to listen with my eyes

Aunt Juanita, I'm sorry I took your silence
as a signal that you had nothing to say
when you spoke in so many ways
crisscrossed crochet needles to your own rhythm

spoke in pastels, oil paints, and canvas
in rocking chair sways and whispers between my cousins
laughing at inside jokes
forming bonds with them I'll never understand

You spoke in American Sign Language
making sure your daughter never felt alone or neglected
then taught her how to speak for herself

You were beautiful
Your voice was softer
like bristles on the end of a paintbrush
Wind could have found freedom in your wavy tresses
but you kept them wound into a bun
Bundled your curves beneath homemade sweaters
Maybe you hid
to save my Gramma the pain
to quiet her comparisons

I think you were her angel
Instead of being the younger sister always cast in her shadow
You were her guardian, never too far behind her steps

In the end, she says you spoke
with the squeeze of her hand
and the fall of a single tear

I think you cried because you knew
how much your big sister
has always needed you

Mi Prima
(for my cousin, Valora)

That night my sister said,
"Her soul was tired of living in her body"

My cousin was the first person I ever saw graduate
Valedictorian with a baby in her arms
before I could appreciate the struggle of a teenage mother
before I was taught to judge anyone for their decisions

I looked up to her, illuminated in expected perfection
a light that shone from both our grandmother's eyes

Valora always seemed to walk on the clouds, above it all
Placed on a pedestal made of our extended arms
each of us on our tippy-toes, pushing her higher

Maybe we pushed too hard
To look upon a disappointed loved one's face
is to attempt suicide on a portion of your soul
And the simple fear of that can eat away at someone
Maybe it was fear

We'll never know
Just as we'll probably never know the truth
of what happened that night
but I believe in my sisters' gift in slumber
and know that you called out, one last time

The pastor said that the body is just a vessel

a container for our spirits
That she's in a better place now
because her spirit has moved on

Hopefully, she's resting
peacefully

J. Holiday

You beckon me to lie down with you
and I nestle myself into your essence
Comfortable like a hamster in the corner of her cage
You make me feel like a baby bird just hatched from its egg
You've gathered soft cotton
from various places to keep me warm
and ensure that I awaken to a world of beautiful colors

You make me feel like royalty
So refined, usually donned in blue shades of satin
and an inviting disposition
Magnetic, everyone who's ever seen you
felt attracted to you, felt compelled to just touch you
You make my 3rd rate,
over-priced-college-student-apartment
feel like home
You are romantic
You're lovely

And, you're a little anti-social...
I don't think we've ever gone out dancing!
But I love you the way you are

You prefer for me to curl up and watch entire seasons
of our favorite shows on television
But I can still walk into the room at 4 am
without you asking any questions
We both know no matter where I go
I'll always come back to you

cause you're so worthwhile

I spent so much time searching for you
my perfect match
When I allowed you into my daily life
my friends told me, you were worth the price
(and they were right)

You were so shy and stubborn
I remember how getting you into the hallway
then into my bedroom left me exhausted
swimming in a pool of my own sweat
and even after all that, you welcomed me

Since then, you've witnessed every version of me
Confident-Vogue, excited-Vogue, self-conscious-Vogue,
depressed-Vogue
If-you-don't-calm-down-Vogue...
hot-ass-morning-breath-havin'-Vogue
take-a-shower-Vogue
and you're-not-walking-out-the-house-
looking-like-that-Vogue

You even tolerate when I throw
objects in your direction without warning
You never seem bothered
by the fact that I refuse to eat at the table
I'd rather sit in your lap
leaving you covered with crumbs
and accidentally spilling drinks on you
I'm sorry

But believe me, I'm grateful

And some days I really miss you
when I'm in my classes I daydream about you
about how you let me melt in your lap like chap-stick
in the pocket of jeans just taken from the dryer
damn near staining you with my body
leaving an imprint of my final position above you
clutching you tightly
ensuring that there is no space
between you and I

You make me feel so…free
I love how sometimes you even allow me
to share you with my friends

and I'm ashamed to say this
because we've been together for 2 years
but I still can't pronounce your name

I guess that's what happens
when you purchase your bed
from that Swedish furniture store, IKEA

Johnny Appleseed

They say we love our sons
and *raise* our daughters
and my brotha?

He's a more mild-mannered kinda guy
Headphones stay huggin' his ears
to keep him from losing his mind

They tell him the only way to be remembered is to:
pick up a ball
sell some dope
call me a bitch
scatter pieces of art across illegal stone canvases
pick up a pen
drop the mic after illuminating
what a broken heart sounds like

He slides his emotions over dope beats and rhymes
on notebooks and scrap paper
Only cries when he can recycle his tears in shot glasses
Smokes weed to exhale his anger
He ain't stupid

He knows this world has very little positivity to deposit
He's selective about the extra voices
he allows to enter his mind
He is still—a piece of serenity
that you know better than to fuck with

And if you asked him, how many women
have tugged at the hem of his heart
just to see how the fibers would fray…?
He'd tell you he's stopped counting

Stopped counting on most women to clear his name:
'cause if her absent father and a good man
stood side by side in a line-up
she wouldn't be able to tell the damn difference

Stopped counting on us
to assist him in his attempt to resurrect chivalry
We tell him, it ain't Lazarus; he ain't Jesus
Chivalry has the stiletto of a 2-inch-black-leather-heel
in the center of its forehead
We did this
Not all of it, but our fingerprints are on the body

So now, he just fucks
because pussy is the only power he can afford
in this recession to validate his masculinity

Where else would you be?
What else can you do
when everyone expects you to fail
doubts your dreams
and laughs at your attempts to fly?

You do what we tell you you're best at:
Pleasing a woman
Even Massa's wife knew there is no substitute

no "battery operated boyfriend"
able to bring a woman to the heights that you can
The simplicity of hearing your success while under her dress
fuels you to continue on to another day

You know that in her arms
between her legs
is the safest place you could ever be

Somethin' embryonic
fetus curled into a woman
breathing synced with hers
This is where you are a king

And if all a woman knows of a man is that they'll leave…
and that the latest [insert-slow-motioned-
baby-oiled-ass-thighs-and-tittied titled] music video
will stop a man mid-conversation with his favorite auntie…

if there's a way to push, pull or swallow
a man into commitment then she will offer this
up on dirty bed sheets freshly spritzed with fabric freshener
or on satin and rose petals
bend over and do it doggy-style
if that's how you want it
cause even if she can't see you
at least she'll be able feel you
press your flesh into her flesh
and attempt to procreate a life
better than what we're livin'

Some men feel like this world cannot hold their greatness
so they scatter themselves amongst many
like Johnny Appleseed, insanity
knowing there are women he cannot trust with his heart
but he'd trust them with his offspring
He says, "at this point, independent women
have some men confused
about what they can offer a woman
other than that good 'D'...
They'll take your time, and your money
but won't take your last name.
They'll suck your dick
but won't swallow their pride to tell us the truth..."

In some ways, he is right...
I wanna start all over, I wanna tell old boyfriends,
"I will always love you
but I never wanted to guide you through this
Most days I don't even know where I'm going...
I just wanted to hold your hand and walk with you"

Men, you are more than battering rams
Ladies, we are more than an open, moist, and soft orifices
We keep trading bodily fluids
small moments of ecstasy
but they always end too quickly
because nothing

can compensate for love
or respect

Eddie Murphy

This poem is about depression
It is about darkness
and closets

Growing up, the only door in my room
was connected to a closet
No such thing as privacy
No doors to lock
No safe space to change in
Nothing to get in trouble for slamming
No way to signal when I wanted to be left alone

I claimed closets "sanctuary"
with night light and good book
Used headphones and fictional fantasies
to muffle domestic earthquakes
fell through cracks landed in a place
where animals have human experiences
Predictable stories assured me that mine
could conclude like theirs
"happy ending" on the Richter scale

Between an abusive mother
a cowardly ghost for a father
a grandmother who holds love for ransom
and a cousin with too many empty post-prison promises
I have cried in dark closets for years

Within dimly lit tears and short-ended tall tales
I discovered an internal mechanism for cheering myself up...
a muscle for working depression out of my system
and Lord knows, I am forced to exercise it often

Even friends claim I have this way of saying
exactly what is needed when it is needed
A way to uplift them and validate what they feel

...until the year that something inside of me cracked
I had nothing to give, so I hid in a dark place
Fear can feel comforted in dark and stormy settings
Remind it that you shine no matter where you are

That shadows don't have depth to fall into
They are empty space
Darkness is empty space
waiting to be filled with something tangible

It wants
children with miniature flashlights
reading "are you afraid of the dark?" bonfire stories

It wants constellations, confession
stripper poles, inappropriate dances moves
in hole-in-the-wall-bars
heated to the exact temperature of booty sweat

It wants love-making, masturbation,
stubbed toes, and a quickie

Wants tears and open hearts
Wants poets writing serious poems
on smart phones past bedtime
It wants to hear "I love you" whispered
from the mouth of an unrequited lover

Wants to watch a child tiptoe through her house
peeking in on her grandmother & older sister
to make sure they are both still breathing
over the sounds of a humidifier

That was me
I get it now

Call me lightning bug
Lotus flower
Viola
Night Owl
Arizona Wildflower

I communicate with my light
I thrive in the mud
I grow best in partial shade
I bloom under moonlight
Nocturnal and wise
See this brown in my skin?
I was made to survive harsh conditions

Give thanks for the darkness
It is the perfect backdrop for light

What They Call You

I know a lot of women who answer to "baby-momma"
in between bitch and slut
Between none-of-yo'-business questions
and open judgmental stares

Answering to that title
feels like answering to perpetual disrespect
feels like no one cares to remember your struggle
that your sacrifice is taken for granted

I even had a guy come into my store
gift shopping for his "moms" and his "babymoms"
I thought to myself, "at least he honors
the mother of his child...amen?"

Lord knows, none of us grew up on fairytale princess movies
and expected to one day be called someone's "baby-momma"
When teachers asked us,
 "What do you wanna be when you grow up?"
"Baby Momma!" was never the response

Pretty soon, when women die, they'll put
"beloved mother, sister, aunt and baby-momma"
on our tombstones

But it's not what they call you
it's what you answer to

Strength of heart is what moves good women
to live outside the labels
and the stench of rotten egg titles
hurled at them from ignorant onlookers
to rise above those names
and only answer to 1: "Mommy"

Mother before bitter
Mother before home-wrecker
Mother before bitch, hoe, slut,
gold-digger, irresponsible, tramp, demon...

Mother: She is responsible for nurturing new life
Courageous
Strong
Wounded
Sacrificing

Men couldn't be baby-mommas if they tried
Women get to make hard choices alone and it's not fair
But there is nothing considerate of a man
who misses the entire gestation period of his child
We accept male disappearance in our communities
like our sons don't learn how to treat women
by observing their fathers
like our futures don't depend on their examples

Instead, some women press forward
waddle across graduation stages
carrying diplomas into new phases of our lives
have our integrity insulted with paternity test requests

trade in extensive wedding plans
for extravagant baby showers
trade in moral support for child support papers
Wanna just get along...
co-operate...
co-parent...
but then wonder if this shit might be easier
if we could just do it alone

Everyone has an opinion on your life-changing decisions
but no one pledges allegiance to baby mommas

At the beginning and end of the day
there is only a woman and her child

The hope of seeing her future in their smiles
Feeling her foundation quake with every kick
Her world is changing
It must change

But she's the only one who felt it

Inheritance

If you've ever received a hug from me
you know it feels like I have separation anxiety
carved into my palms
I squeeze too hard
I really can't tell you when this began
but what I can tell you, is that his name was Robert Garnett

He had a bushy mustache, hinted with flecks of grey
He smelled like cigarettes and laundry detergent
Stood at 5 feet 10 inches; 160 pounds
Insecure about his skinny legs
so he wore sweatpants under his jeans
He was the poster child of well-kept taco meat chest hair

Leftovers from unattended acne, his cheeks were smooth
but looked like the surface of a pumice stone
My sister called him crater face
Gramma said she didn't trust him

But I remember inheriting my mother's admiration
He was a man, her man in the midst of a custody battle
he held her close, her sergeant at arms
Led our bible studies giving us a home
that prayed together
I watched football with him on Sundays
and he explained the rules

Robert was well-traveled, well-read
He lifted weights regularly
I remember barely being able to bench press

the bar he put the weights on

One night, he made me stay up past my bedtime
offended that I had never seen the movie "Stand By Me"
I still haven't

He touched me
The way a man should never touch a 13-year-old
Fondled beneath pink panties with un-manicured fingers
Lifted up oversized night shirt
to place sloppy tongue
across navel and nipples
across non-existent breasts

Lips poured out words to petrify organs
with a smile he asked, "Did you like it?
Does that feel good?"
I nodded
Rewound my life to recited statistics:

"Roughly 33% of girls and 14% of boys are molested
before the age of 18...More than 50% of molestation and
rapes are committed by someone the survivor knows...
It is often a family member or close friend...In most cases
child molestation goes unreported. It is not okay.
It is never your fault."
It is not okay
It is never your fault
It is not okay

It is never your fault

My mind pressed 'Play':

Pulling my shirt down and my underwear up
I scurried into my room
Pathetically pressed my plastic chair
against the door at an adjacent angle

I remember writing out every detail
in my pink and blue Tweety Bird diary
and placing it into my mother's purse

The same diary that kept my secrets
about crushes on boys at school
Lee Thompson Young and the lyrics
to my favorite Destiny's Child song: "Bills Bills Bills"

I knew she'd read the whole thing
But I had watched enough after school specials
to know that this was not something you stayed silent about

She came home from work in a blur
Eyes swollen, she asked me, "Are you sure?
Robert said he did some of those things,
but that you made up the rest.
Are you sure?"

He came out of their bedroom smiling at me,
"Now Vogue, you know you press up against me.
Even the elders at church talk about how you
squeeze them too tightly. We talked about this."
And to this day, my mother refuses to talk about it
I guess the words feel as uncomfortable in her mouth

as his hands felt between my legs
So she pretends like it never happened

Like she didn't bring me a dictionary the next day
and have me look up rape, incest,
and molestation, then tell me to choose which one
best categorized our "situation"

Like she didn't tell me to get used to telling the story
over...and over...and over again
because that's what I'd have to do in courtrooms

Like for two years,
I ain't live under the same roof of this man
while a drug addiction stole my mother

In 2009, I found out he died of cancer

While Chemotherapy robbed him of his appetite
My mother spoon-fed him love until his final breath

In a corner of the studio apartment
she rents in Los Angeles
there is a table with a framed photo of him
A small shrine
A memento of his importance to her

When you greet me accept my hugs as proof
that I am bruised, not broken

That surviving is a lot harder
than curling into a ball
praying to disappear

Content

The edges of our lie-laden love letters
cut deeper into my fingertips with time
and yet I keep on reading them

Maybe, it is our letters' desire
to be dyed a passionate hue
to be washed free of the sin
we dipped them in

See, I think our love letters are comparing
my love for you to that of Christ's
because I feel like I've been sacrificing blood for you

Every night my wounded fingertips dance
choreographed calligraphy across our letters
with the same three words:
                    IMISSYOU
i-miss-you
I Miss You

I'm tempted to etch my signature
onto the last page of our letters
the same way I tried to scratch my initials
into your back when we made love

I wanna bite the upper left-hand corner of our letters
stapling them together — leaving my teeth marks
for her to compare to that scar I left
on your left shoulder

I wanna envelop our letters in the disdain I have for you
seal it with a kiss goodbye
Take it to my sister, my cousin, my grandma
and my closest friends to stamp with their disapproval
And then I wanna mail them to you
Cause I'm tired of looking at them

It's your turn
Your turn to cry acidic tears
that burn your face obvious with sorrow

Those tears you swear you cry
every time you get a chance to pry yourself from her

You swear she was never anything to you, a nobody
"just a warm body"
and me, the love of your "sorry-ass-life"
is 1,443 miles away
All you need is time
You'll get yourself together
and we'll be together
I'll see! We have interlocking destinies

Please stop mapquesting misinformation

It's not like you're going to come, visit, and reimburse
the $2,500 you owe me for your freedom
We both know where you stand
and we both know I already stood by your side
But you chose someone to coddle you

like the baby you imitate instead of the woman
who would help you stand on your feet
like the man you're afraid to become

I'm done

I've been plaguing my poetry with your presence
and it really deserves deeper content than this
So tonight, I pray this poem
be my form of self-exorcism
because you've possessed me
for too long

The Ramblings of a Fearful Woman

Is this real? Or just a quick fix for the both of us?
I'm wondering how long this will last
Actually, I'm wondering
how long I will allow this to last

I know I'm not ready to make someone my everything again
I don't wanna meet your family
share dinner conversations and smiles with them
while attempting to gain their approval
and prove we can share you, too

I don't wanna bring you to open mics
intrigue you with my stage presence
have you meet my poetry family
and give you yet another reason to like me...

I'm somewhere in the middle
I desire to be loved
held tightly
nestled beneath your chin
comforted by your warmth
that will melt away my insecurities...

I want you to be my refuge
I want to have that physical connection with you
But I'm afraid I'll be pressured into intercourse
in six months without the promise of a deep interconnection
Love
because affection is not enough

I'm scared of the risk of being hurt
toyed with like a child's plaything
some item that is discarded
when a younger, faster, more expensive model
comes into view
only to be revisited in memories of "the good ole days"

Can you stay true?
Care for me enough to keep me in good condition?
Will you tend to my scratches? Add a few patches?
I promise I'll do the same for you
And dare I say it?
Marriage

Promise me marriage!
Not that it means much nowadays
Check the divorce rates
The infidelity
The lost-and-found deep-rooted secrets
Excuse me for being a pessimist
Sometimes, I'm a realist
Hope for the best, prepare for the worst
Bury me head first before I step
into anybody's white dress without a prenup

I'm just, a firm believer
in the idea that people change
It's sometimes called growth, but that growth
may or may not be what's best for "us"
so please, just leave…

I've been basing my decisions in fear
since the possibility of heartbreak was made clear

I can already see us in the last months of matrimony
mindlessly going through our daily routines:
"good morning"
"good night"
breakfast, lunch, and dinner in between
award-worthy actors in a perfect family scene...until:

One day you'll be at work
I'll be at home, faithful housewife
just finished sorting through our 17-year-old son's clothing
I'll move on to bedclothes
and find, hidden within the linens
your lipstick-stained-and-perfumed shirt, so cliché...

I'll toss it into the dry cleaning pile
sort through my tears
blurred vision still making out
images of our marriage
as it unravels
in the cotton fibers
one color at a time...

He asked, "What are you thinking?"

And she answered, truthfully

Ellipses

We never wished to be born
We wish for nuclear families
on shooting stars against pitch black midnight skies
hoping for a real existence
We close the ends of sentences with certainty, periods

We are the end results of premature acts
Survivors of unexcused absences

Born to Fathers, maybe
who pay child support
rarely pay visits
Mothers
who pound the importance of education
into our minds the same way
their boyfriends pounded them into walls
Mothers
who wrestled with their own white lines
kept us close to home
learned us how to live in this world, but not of it
Mothers
swollen like question marks
we are the stillborn answers to every question
they were bursting to ask, but never did

They remained pregnant with guilt
Gave birth to hushed secrets of identity
"Did you see her? How old is she?
Who tha Daddy? Oh my!"

We are the dots completing their exclamation points

We were told no beautiful tales of our conception
No parents' fingers accidentally grazed as they tried
to scoop up over-priced college textbooks
from cemented walkways
or syrupy-sweethearts stuck together since high school

Our families keep secrets that don't belong to them
confining truth beneath their tongues like razors
They watch us cut ourselves
Watch us pretend to be fairies
We sprinkle hope dust in the form of blood tests
to verify our existence
Pray for someone to put their hands together
and say they believe in us

We are fragments of history
Puzzle pieces of truth living within the whispers
of broken vows
of scattered half-siblings found
and lost and found
and lost again in the wind

We are sons
who learn to tie our ties
with no daddies
We are arms
emptied, left to give
ourselves away at wedding ceremonies
We are mature daughters

who double as best friends
to insecure mothers
We are questions
replaced with rage
too angry to concentrate in classes
then labeled with ADHD

We are left on the sides of dumpsters
outside orphanages
in toilets

We are left on old patio porches
bent plywood creaking beneath our weight, unstable
moving from foster home
to foster home
our true beauty never fostered

And will we have children?
Maybe
Maybe not

We often find ourselves
in the corresponding stories of others
some, resilient
some, fallen by the wayside

Sometimes we are left in sets of three
periods side by side, ellipses
the unfinished potential of our parents…

You Only Said Goodbye with Words
(For Amy Winehouse)

I denied your death
pretended you were somewhere strumming Cherry
fading to Black, writing music
in your bathrobe on a kitchen floor
wearing fuck me pumps

Didn't follow the funeral procession
to see who paid homage…
until Bruno Mars covered your version of "Valerie"
Did you hear it?

When I was in college, I prescribed your songs
like medication for broken hearts
Built friendships on the foundation of your lyrics
Created an online group called
"Yes-yes-yes to Amy Winehouse"
Knowing that I'd have to sacrifice
your art, my salvation
to save your life

I wish you would've sat with yourself long enough
and found your beauty
Taken off the make-up seen simplicity
Unpinned the hive and realized you're the queen
who threw her heart down a wishing well

You were Frank and honesty is so taboo…so intriguing
that Prince wanted you to come on tour with him

Jay-Z did a verse over Rehab
You referred to K-os as Kevin
You performed onstage with Mos-Def
after making a random request
'Round midnight, you still hold me close
when my ex-boyfriends won't

You were jazz and hip-hop
Best of both words
British and Improper
You were low cut necklines, high cut skirts, stick figure
honey beehive hair, tattoos crawling up your arms
During interviews you were gum smacking, cracking jokes
bra straps showing... Amy, you were such a fucking mess
and Tony Bennett called you a true Jazz singer
how tragic that you left in their tradition

You should've gone to rehab a 4th time
for that fucked up relationship you were in

A 5th time...
but you should've done it your way
should've locked yourself in a padded room
with your band of choice
should've had jam sessions,
recorded your "Me Against The World" album
composed of freedom songs
What does withdrawal sound like?
You'd probably be the only one to paint it perfect in melody

Some of us artists can't hold onto ourselves

when it's our self-appointed duty to share
every ounce of truth in our veins and repair the hearts
of anyone who is willing listen
Some of us just can't do this shit while sober
Physicians can heal themselves, not artists

Your body became a stranger
once your thighs stopped touching
In Serbia, the crowd watched you spin barefoot
and sloppy during that concert
attempting pirouettes in drunken stupor
the only noise they could conjure
from their greedy diaphragms was discontent
Boo's that probably still echoed in your ears when you
swayed off stage...
It was the moment the pain looked too real
When the sound of your bones clicking together
became loud enough for the microphone to pick up
Your voice drowned out by the alcohol rolling
in the deep of your stomach

You see, Amy, it's okay to self-destruct on-stage
as long as it's still entertaining

How did they forget you were human?
Why didn't anyone give you more than their ears and eyes?
Why didn't someone give you their hands...
tell you to be okay...
that everything would be okay?
Attempt to crawl onstage to sing with you?

A few days later you joined
Brian Jones, Alan Wilson, Jimi Hendrix,
Janis Joplin, Kurt Cobain, Jim Morrison...

I never saw you in concert, let you know you changed my life
Never made a bucket-list and placed you on it
Never said thank you for making me feel comfortable
about being rough around the edges
It never seemed urgent

Amy, what if I never write that poem that heals me?
I don't want to die like Mozart writing his last composition
I don't want to die at age twenty-seven
within the confines of these pages
I need my life to be more meaningful

I want to bake cookies and make cinna-nutmeg pancakes
Chaperone field trips, kiss boo-boos
write poems for my niece and my sister
I don't want to die and have them mourn me
the way a fan mourns an idol

But Amy, I promise to write
until there are no more songs left in me
Promise to perform poetry I'd want to hear
Promise to attend more concerts
Promise to write things I have problems with
and get past them
I will make something good out of the bad

I promise to enjoy every moment I spend on a stage

To be thankful that the audiences I perform in front of
will snap their fingers in support of my heart
instead of rounding their mouths
to jeer at my breathing corpse

My bucket-list will still include your voice
I'll hear you play
maybe perform beside you at heaven's gate
maybe God will let us both in,
just to give the mourners whose other halves didn't make it
something to listen to

A prescription to subdue their broken hearts

Afterword

Vogue 3:16?

You know…there's a Christian bible verse…
"For God so loved the world that he gave his only begotten Son, that whosoever believeth in him should not perish, but have everlasting life" (John 3:16).

This particular bible verse confounded my brain for years. I remember being in church as a kid and wondering, "Why would God, the all-powerful, choose to give up his only immaculately conceived child to show his love and give us everlasting life?"

However, as an avid reader, I came to love stories like this. Stories where maybe the point isn't in the literal translation, but in the concept itself. Maybe the lesson in God's action was to show an example of love as sacrifice. I mean, romantic love is cute and all, but love as sacrifice is a heavy concept. To give up a part of yourself, so that another part can live.

I'm not claiming to be a prophet, nor a priestess. Heck, I'm not even claiming a full-time religion. If God was evaluating my faith, he'd label me lukewarm and spit me up outta his mouth. I've known this since my first smidge of doubt and deliberate disobedience of a Christian biblical commandment. Some days, this makes me sad…and a little fearful, you know, with hell looming over and under my psyche.

I try not to think about it.

If the world's religions came together in one room and cooked up a smorgasbord, you would find me with too many morals and beliefs on my plate. I'd like to believe I'll be reincarnated into the type of bird that flies south for the winter (preferably one that mankind doesn't hunt). Or maybe salmon…yea, salmon.

I'd like to believe that Jesus enjoyed celebrations of life and eating good food. That sometimes, he believed a day deserved more wine, less water. I believe my sister has psychic abilities and so does my polishing buddy. I'd like to think that when babies are having conversations with mid-air, all smiley, (and they aren't gassy) they are talking to their angels.

I know that suffering is a part of life and when I fully understood that, I found a better sense of inner peace. I know that after fasting for a day during Ramadan, I appreciated life and the abundance I have access to. I know that science can link depression to the amount of sunlight a person is getting and have found myself arms outstretched to the sun, gleefully absorbing its warmth. I believe we are made of star stuff...of atoms and everything has mass. I know that if a group of women are around each other too often, their menstrual cycles sync up and it's bloody ridiculous. However, this proves how much of an effect we have on each other. I believe in responsibility.

I heard that my grandma cursed the Christian God on the day her mother passed away. I know my great aunt and uncle had a love so strong, they died within one month of each other. Sometimes, your partner is the only thing that keeps you alive.

I believe in the power of positive thoughts, of manifesting your dreams by saying them aloud as catalyst and engine. This is no different than prayer. It's just semantics.

I have been brought to tears in spoken word venues. Have rocked myself into "okay" after being so heavily moved by someone's story. Strangely, the most consistent place I have felt the Holy Spirit has been in a spoken word venue. Guess that explains why my favorite part of church has always been when the pastor steps away from the pulpit and allows the congregation to shine light on their faith by giving testimonies.

Why the title Vogue 3:16?
Name: Vogue Martine Robinson
Birthdate: March 16, 1987

About the Author

Born in Phoenix, AZ
Raised in Perris, CA
Grew up in Los Angeles, CA

Vogue will always have an appreciation for human beings who find ways to put truth and heart into words. She was introduced to Spoken Word by her friend, Nicole, while in college at San Diego State University. She was apprehensive to share any of her written work to others, but soon the audience became part of the reason why she performed. Spoken Word brings a new element to her writing.

She currently resides in Las Vegas, Nevada. If you are interested in booking her for a performance in your city, please email voguerobinson@gmail.com .

When she's not writing, she's spending time with her niece or sitting in math classes and tutoring awesome children.

To keep up with Vogue, you can find her artist page on facebook under "Vogue Robinson".

Praise for Vogue 3:16

"Beautifully written. Soulful, candid, and warm. This book of poetry puts words to paper the way Mama cooks. No measurements, no recipes, does so with a knowledge that surpasses what is taught   in school and to a method all her own. A body of work that can never be emulated because you won't be able to get it to "taste" just right. A beautiful spirit is transfixed within these pages. Only by reading it, do you feel this divine presence. Written for a spectrum of women, from most every facet of life. We all have been that young girl, that young lady, and aspire to be that woman in some form or fashion. Open your eyes to allow this wonderful voice in. With every page you are moved. Allow yourself to experience an earthquake, you won't be the only one who felt it."

-Shea Ellis, Writer and Avid Reader

"Vogue 3:16 is similar to reading a biography and a Bible wrapped into one. The poetry is so full of her life and essence that when you read it, you hear her reciting it inside your head (even if you've never met her). It is also an emotional roller coaster, and even if you hate roller coasters, you want to ride this one. From her first line to her last she takes you to a place so beautiful that she inspires you to become more. I laughed, cried, and felt at home reading her poetry. She is an amazing writer. Vogue 3:16 is her introduction to you and is a hug that lasts a second too long, but you don't mind."

-Ami Rebecca Meyers, Avid Reader

"Vogue 3:16 is an elaborate metaphor that transcends all aspects of Vogue Robinson's personality. Her unique poetic style is showcased in all of her poems and she conveys her deepest emotions with her readers. With brilliant humor, she is able to discuss the most serious matters in a light-hearted way. The afterword of her book reads like a diary entry, very personal and candid. Her carefree personality shows throughout as she discusses the purpose behind her title, which is reflective of her spirituality and the understanding of it.

As the poetry begins, Robinson entertains her readers with her beautiful words and unique storytelling skills. Throughout her book, readers are introduced to not only her thoughts, but to her family, friends, mentors and past romantic relationships. Robinson's honesty is a breath of fresh air to all who are seeking to hear their story to be told."

-Brianna N. Bennett, MPA, Education Professional

About The Publisher

WRAGS Ink. is a family-run publishing company based in New York, California and Pennsylvania. We provide a solid partnership working with determined writers looking to gain a foothold in the literary world.

We focus on the novice, the hobbyist and the semi-professional creator offering services ranging from fiction to nonfiction, educational to quirky.

For more information about the company and how to get your work discovered, visit www.wragsink.com

$5 Coupon!

By purchasing this book, you are entitled to a discount on "Vogue 3:16" non-print products (cd, t-shirts, etc.). Please email voguerobinson@gmail.com for further details on your discount! This is Vogue's little way of saying, "thank you" to the readers.